Send an email to du@dianeupdyke.com,
and write in the subject line:
"Consulting Inquiry."
'm happy to answer the first question from my
own knowledge bank or discuss engagements
if it's a longer dialogue.
I look forward to connecting.

Building Your Sales Team

Beyond People, Process, and Technology

Diane Updyke

An Actionable Sales Journal
with Useful Inspirations

E-mail: info@thinkaha.com
20660 Stevens Creek Blvd., Suite 210
Cupertino, CA 95014

Published by THiNKaha®
20660 Stevens Creek Blvd., Suite 210, Cupertino, CA 95014
http://thinkaha.com
E-mail: info@thinkaha.com

Photography by Jlee Studio 9

First Printing: April 2019
Hardcover ISBN: 978-1-61699-317-7   1-61699-317-0
Paperback ISBN: 978-1-61699-316-0   1-61699-316-2
eBook ISBN: 978-1-61699-315-3   1-61699-315-4
Place of Publication: Silicon Valley, California, USA
Paperback Library of Congress Number: 2018967994

Trademarks

All terms mentioned in this book that are known to be trademarks or service marks have been appropriately capitalized. Neither THiNKaha, nor any of its imprints, can attest to the accuracy of this information. Use of a term in this book should not be regarded as affecting the validity of any trademark or service mark.

Warning and Disclaimer

Every effort has been made to make this book as complete and as accurate as possible. The information provided is on an "as is" basis. The author(s), publisher, and their agents assume no responsibility for errors or omissions. Nor do they assume liability or responsibility to any person or entity with respect to any loss or damages arising from the use of information contained herein.

Acknowledgement

First, to the leaders and explorers who taught me Sales and Marketing Alignment until it was a rote part of my existence, plus the many companies and clients who let me practice so I can now sense when it's right.

Second, to all the Sales Support teams, who make all the Vice Presidents of Sales look better than we are. To Ops, who can create the speed that our minds can analyze; to Sales Enablement, who takes a sales team and gets it to hum; to Sales Development, who the key to filling the funnel and navigating the nuances between marketing and sales.

Third, to the Contributors who were eager to share their knowledge; the Contributors who didn't know they could find the words, but did; and to the Contributors who really wanted to give their wisdom but couldn't craft it into a quick message (you have so much to say and we'll cull it for next time). I say, thank you. Different voices always make any product better. Let's keep sharing.

Dedication

To my hubby, who has the best strategic and political mind I know. He helps me look at what's next.

To my daughter, who navigates socially and educationally the current world in ways I never could. She can break down issues into basic principles and geometric shapes so I can look at them simply. She should be in sales but doesn't know it yet.

To my mom, because she and my dad taught me what it's like to maintain healthy relationships.

low to Read a THiNKaha® Book

Note from the Publisher

1e AHAthat/THiNKaha series is the CliffsNotes of the 21st
ntury. These books are contextual in nature. Although the
tual words won't change, their meaning will every time you read
1e as your context will change. Be ready, you will experience
ur own AHA moments as you read the AHA messages™ in this
ok. They are designed to be stand-alone actionable messages
at will help you think about a project you're working on, an
ent, a sales deal, a personal issue, etc. differently. As you read
is book, please think about the following:

It should only take 15–20 minutes to read this book the first
time out. When you're reading, write in the underlined area
one to three action items that resonate with you.

Mark your calendar to re-read this book again in 30 days.

Repeat step #1 and mark one to three more AHA messages that
resonate. They will most likely be different than the first time.
BTW: this is also a great time to reflect on the AHA messages
that resonated with you during your last reading.

fter reading a THiNKaha book, marking your AHA messages,
-reading it, and marking more AHA messages, you'll begin
see how these books contextually apply to you. AHAthat/
HiNKaha books advocate for continuous, lifelong learning.
1ey will help you transform your AHAs into actionable items
.th tangible results until you no longer have to say AHA to
ese moments—they'll become part of your daily practice as
ou continue to grow and learn.

itchell Levy, The AHA Guy at AHAthat
1blisher@thinkaha.com

Contents

Introduction

When you're stuck with your team's current habits, when y
wonder how to inspire your team next, when you want someo
else's wisdom/humor/thoughts, then come on over here. Y
have knowledge and data, but sometimes, it's hard to conju
new ideas from them. However, one can judge and gut check
something is right/wrong for their own situation.

I have over twenty years of beliefs, tips, and practices. We g
to build our lessons from our own cringeworthy mistakes, th
mistakes of others, and the valuable lessons our managers besto
like a gift. It is a blessing to learn from the rungs of others, a
I have from the managers before me. And I've had really goo
ones. You will get to hear from a few here.

There is input from many roles: VPS, CMOs, CEOs, VCs, SD
mgrs., and great reps. Inside is part science, part diligence, pa
art, part emotional intelligence, and part market awareness. It's
tough job to manage a system and motivate an individual. No
multiply those nuances by 20 or 100, and that's the job of th
manager: to help the ecosystem rise to success, to get 75 perce
of your reps to succeed, to create a culture of predictability. Yo
are Zeus . . . or Athena? Nah. We'll just be humans who simp
plug away.

I've gone through the trajectory of having a customer tell me (
the early days), "You seem mad at us because we won't buy."
cringed. It was true. It should be, "I am buying from you becau:
I know your team will be there for the changes."

Everyone gets stuck in their own thoughts and the habits
the current process. We can be slaves to a methodology we'
enlisted, as we try to instill a regiment. Know what? Sometime
we need someone else as a sounding board or inspiration so w

n quit thinking and then feel for a moment, learn from another's
rbiage, and get comical inspiration to disrupt the team. That's
l this does. You *know* what do. You want a little inspiration, a
w idea, or a catchphrase to amuse the troops.

u don't have to read this in sequence. Take a random page, take
1 appropriate subject, take wisdom from a leader you'd like to
1ow, and co-opt the crap out of their stuff.

lways say about sales calls that one has to inform or entertain,
   look at the cycle from the customer's POV. Sometimes, the
cret is to glean the customer's POV. Do you really know what
ey're thinking? Keep reading. I have a magic question that
u can ask at every meeting—it never gets old and gives you a
rprising depth of answers 100 percent of the time.

Prospects buy out of hope or fear. Some buy hoping to solve their vision while others buy fearing that they won't be in style if they don't buy a new product.
#Sales

Diane Updyke
http://aha.pub/BuildingYourSalesTeam

Share the AHA messages from this book socially by going to
http://aha.pub/BuildingYourSalesTeam

Section 1

It's the Customer, Basically

The Customer needs to become your passion: how you talk to them, how you become valuable to them, how you invest in their success, etc. This section reveals how to learn the messaging that engages them and the general strategies that can frame your sales cycles.

Watch this video:
http://aha.pub/BuildingYourSalesTeamS1

1

Marketing manifests the messaging, direction, and consistency. #Sales proves if it's true or false.

_____

_____

_____

2

#Sales is the best distribution channel for marketing content. Their social network can be up to 20x that of your company's, making it the most targeted and prolific megaphone for your marketing message.
—Kurt Shaver (CSO of Vengreso)
via Diane Updyke

_____

_____

_____

3

Don't tell prospects (or anyone) why you're great. Learn what they want to hear because it will tie to what they care about. #Sales

_____

_____

_____

4

Your number one competitive differentiator is the results you drive for your customers. —John Barrows (CEO of JBarrows Sales Training) via Diane Updyke

_____

_____

_____

5

Find what captures your prospect's head
and heart. What do you want them to know
and feel after the meeting? #Sales

_____

_____

_____

6

People want to be entertained and informed with data, examples, and vision. Are you entertaining and informing your prospects? #Sales

_____

_____

_____

7

Take a big glug from the reality cup to define your sales goals. Ask yourself the hard question: Are you a vitamin or an aspirin? When you have the answer, plan accordingly. —Trish Bertuzzi (President of The Bridge Group, Inc.) via Diane Updyke

_____

_____

_____

8

Don't let the facts get in the way of a good story. Build a story for them that captures their vision—of what they can become. #Sales

_____

_____

_____

9

Sales execs want you to sell value, but to sell value, you need to know the customer's problem, to know the problem they have to trust you, and to earn value, you have to build a relationship. It all starts with relationships.
—Paul Teshima (CEO of Nudge.ai)
via Diane Updyke

_____

_____

10

If you act like the founder or a large shareholder in the company, strategic decisions become clearer with respect to your role and impact.
—Ryan Floyd (Managing Director of Storm Ventures) via Diane Updyke

_____

_____

11

Prospects buy out of hope or fear. Some buy hoping to solve their vision, while others buy fearing that they won't be in style if they don't buy a new product. #Sales

_____

_____

_____

12

Marketers HOPE you can solve their problem; Technology Buyers DARE you to.

_____

_____

_____

13

Selling to "hope" is matching the vision on high with current project plans and environment at the departmental level. #Sales

_____

_____

_____

14

Selling to "fear" means a prospect is just "dipping a toe in." They want to try it out with minimal disruption to resources, and they need more proof of ROI. #Sales

_____

_____

_____

15

Selling into enterprise deals or into new markets are best served with a two-prong sales approach — one has the strategy, while another has the problem. #Sales

_____

_____

_____

16

Are you a hero to your boss and to your reports? Ask yourself regularly how you can serve others.

_____

_____

_____

One metric like ARR or CAC does not drive your business — you need to take the time to understand the business. Too many people look for shortcuts, — and that leads to a lack of understanding and poor decision making.
—Ryan Floyd (Managing Director of Storm Ventures)

Diane Updyke
http://aha.pub/BuildingYourSalesTeam

Share the AHA messages from this book socially by going to
http://aha.pub/BuildingYourSalesTeam

Section II

Are Your Goals Steady?

Every board wants you, as a Start-up Leader, to fire on multiple cylinders, but that can be distracting. Focus on one key tenet for the business as it needs to be for the next one to two years. Even as your business grows, you still have to narrow your actions around a subset from all the lofty goals. Here is how to find that focus and the surrounding metrics.

Watch this video:
http://aha.pub/BuildingYourSalesTeamS2

17

Decide on a single priority. Which one is the most important? Is it the customer logo, max revenue, minimal churn, or profit? #Sales

_____

_____

_____

18

Reconcile how the propect views your solution vs. how you value your need for recurring revenue. Do they see you as a campaign or as an ongoing solution?

_____

_____

_____

19

Do not count a trial as a deal; it's a POC and not a commitment for long-term customer value.

_____

_____

_____

20

You can measure many things; but it's hard to manage more than 5 key metrics. Direct your team to what is most important and not to every measurement you have.

_____

_____

_____

21

Numbers help you find where you suck so you can evaluate yourself, adjust your goals, and get better! #Progress

_____

_____

_____

22

One metric like ARR or CAC does not drive your business—you need to take the time to understand the business. Too many people look for shortcuts, and that leads to a lack of understanding and poor decision making. —Ryan Floyd (Managing Director of Storm Ventures) via Diane Updyke

_____

_____

_____

23

Set goals for Customer Acquisition Costs
(CAC) once you have repeatable sales and
an identifiable Ideal Customer Profile (ICP).
Prior to that, you're just arguing
about expenses.

_____

_____

_____

24

Investors will set goals for startups to produce 5-7x on-target earnings (OTE) per rep. Reality for most early stagers is closer to 3-5x OTE, so don't feel down.

_____

_____

_____

What I've learned is the greater your personal awareness, the more effective you are as a Salesperson. Neutrality, listening, connecting to what a customer needs — to do that well requires high EQ. — Joe Hubbard (Director of Trainings at Thrive Global)

Diane Updyke
http://aha.pub/BuildingYourSalesTeam

Share the AHA messages from this book socially by going to
http://aha.pub/BuildingYourSalesTeam

Section III

Developing Your Sales Model and Organizing Your Chaos

Welcome to the meat of the matter. Developing or modifying a sales model is part science (from those who came before you) and part art (your specific industry, at your stage, at this particular time). Either way, you have to start somewhere. So do your reps. Here are the mechanics of building a repeatable sales model. Also, tie it up in a formula for meeting your number consistently.

Watch this video:
http://aha.pub/BuildingYourSalesTeamS3

25

Enterprise selling has a fashion pendulum; it gets you named customers and better revenue-for-effort, while Small and Midsized businesses (SMB) get you logos. Both are good.

_____

_____

_____

26

Historically, Enterprise selling is justified around $50K ARR because it covers the cost of selling and justifies the resources used.

_____

_____

_____

27

The difference between Enterprise and
Midmarket selling is how you prospect, how
many people you have to touch, and how the
relationships you build expand businesses
to other departments.

_____

_____

_____

28

I've been told by Marketing execs of
Enterprise accounts that #Sales has to talk
to 15 people in their org to close a deal—
from interest to signature.

_____

_____

_____

29

To close a deal for SMBs, we have to talk to at least 3 contacts in an org. For VSB (Very Small Business), you better close it with 1.

_____

_____

_____

30

Technology minimizes what a rep has to do. Discipline helps reps focus on the selling activities they should do.

_____

_____

_____

31

Your two best time investments prior to being in front of a prospect are preparation and practice.

_____

_____

_____

32

Two-thirds of a representative's time is spent on non-selling activities. Managing a rep's time is a stifling culture. Teach and motivate them to manage their own time. Teach them to fish!

_____

_____

_____

33

Just like you should inspect your car parts and engine systems every six months, check up on your CRM methodology, time management practices, and interdepartmental communication paths.

_____

_____

_____

34

While managers are there to offer strategy and guidance, don't rob your team of the ability to learn from mistakes. It's okay to learn.

_____

_____

_____

35

What I've learned is the greater your personal awareness, the more effective you are as a Salesperson. Neutrality, listening, connecting to what a customer needs — to do that well requires high EQ.
—Joe Hubbard (Director of Trainings Thrive Global) via Diane Updyke

---

36

Emotional Intelligence is the capability of individuals to recognize their own emotions, those of others, and prioritize how to talk to others' over theirs.

37

First impressions matter. Invest in a great connection, make sure to research and KNOW who your prospect is BEFORE reaching out. —MariAnne Vanella (CEO of The Vanella Group, Inc.) via Diane Updyke

---

38

Up to 50% of a rep's business are customers who were nurtured 18 months ago. That's a fact that will keep Enterprise reps developing relationships.

39

Pick up the phone first, email last. Don't be afraid to have an engaging conversation. Warm calls are good, but great salespeople love making the cold call.
—Neil Callahan (Co-founder of Pilot Growth Equity) via Diane Updyke

_____

_____

_____

40

Without an agenda to set the stage for a meeting, the client is in control, you're not. —John Barrows (CEO of JBarrows Sales Training) via Diane Updyke

_____

_____

_____

41

If you can teach only one thing, teach the reps how to ask the right questions.

_____

_____

_____

42

The right questions are those that a) move the deal, b) uncover hidden info, c) find more players, or d) release the Kraken of obstacles.

_____

_____

_____

43

My favorite question EVER: What of what we talked about today resonated the most? The answer will surprise you 99% of the time.

_____

_____

_____

44

You can tell how well a rep will do in price negotiations by reviewing the quality of their discovery.
—Matt Cameron (Sales Management Program Leader of SaaSy Sales Management) via Diane Updyke

_____

_____

_____

45

Discovery is NOT a one-time conversation with one person. Triangulate what you've learned with other key stakeholders. It builds your value proposition, sells larger deals, and solves real business problems.
—Debe Rapson (Enterprise Director, Sprinklr) via Diane Updyke

_____

_____

_____

46

Ask AT LEAST three times in different ways,
What are the challenges keeping you from
achieving your initiatives?" It's amazing what
you'll uncover when you dig deeper.
—Debe Rapson (Enterprise Director
at Sprinklr) via Diane Updyke

_____

_____

_____

47

Discovery is the art of creating a conversation,
never selling, but sharing relevant stories of
similar customer experiences while learning
what you need to know to bring value
to a customer's business.
—Debe Rapson (Enterprise Director, Sprinklr)
via Diane Updyke

_____

_____

_____

48

Discovery calls are a thing of the past. You can pre-qualify people using BANT with information openly available via internet. Chat bots killed lead forms, since you qualify people right there on the spot when you have their attention.
—Max Altschuler (VPM of Outreach.io) via Diane Updyke

_____

_____

49

A Sales Methodology is to enlighten prospects and knock aside competition.

_____

_____

_____

50

How many methodologies do you speak? I've used 6. The Magic is consistency and common language. Eventually, you'll roll your own.

_____

_____

_____

51

Your methodology will improve EVERY TIME you run into a repeated obstacle.

_____

_____

_____

52

Use what you know about your prospect, and be relevant & personal in your quest for the pain. Don't forget to twist the knife when setting up the business case on why they should do business with you.
—Debe Rapson (Enterprise Director, Sprinklr) via Diane Updyke

_____

_____

_____

53

The Goal is a repeatable sales model. Again, the Goal is a repeatable sales model, NOT religious purity.

_____

_____

_____

54

The sales process starts with finding your ICP and tiering your low-hanging fruit. The best sales pitch in the world on the wrong audience will fall flat. ICP is the #1 most important piece of your process.
—Max Altschuler (VPM of Outreach.io) via Diane Updyke

_____

_____

_____

55

The sales model works when you can get to quota with B players. Everyone wants A-only players. That luxury doesn't last if you continue to grow and test.

_____

_____

56

The #1 mistake sales development leaders make when building compensation plans is forcing their reps to choose between what's good for the rep and what's good for the company.
—Taft Love (Global Director of SmartRecruiters) via Diane Updyke

_____

_____

_____

57

Companies that "peanut butter spread"
quotas across similar roles see 14% less
quota attainment than those that stagger
quotas according to territory opportunity
(make it a fair fight).
—Chris Cabrera (CEO, Xactly Corp.)
via Diane Updyke

_____

_____

_____

58

Which comes first, the model or the sales plays? The models are tested formats for selling. The sales plays are company-specific words for your industry, product, prospect, and competitive landscape.

_____

_____

_____

59

Across multiple SaaS organizations, sales teams close approx. 30% of the deals forecasted to close in any given quarter. The spread has been 28%-33%. It's a tight cluster.

_____

_____

_____

60

Practically, I have found Enterprise Sales Reps can manage about 15 deals at various stages in any given quarter. Xactly shows data that Enterprise reps will close 13 deals per year.

_____

_____

_____

61

Most businesses have seasonality. Your quotas should be too. A typical example for SaaS quarterly quotas is 27%-29%-23%-31%. Just kidding, that's 110%, which is what a leader hopes for. It's really more like: 25%-27%-19%-29%, assuming a calendar year.

_____

_____

_____

62

You may get up to 50% of your current business from companies you prospected to 18 months ago. A true statistic. Happened to my team at a large Martech company.

_____

_____

_____

63

We are 31% more productive when we are in a positive mindset. Look for people who are motivated by positivity, they will absolutely produce more! —Joe Hubbard (Director of Trainings at Thrive Global) via Diane Updyke

_____

_____

_____

64

Always Have a Plan B. When do you EVER get to finish a month or quarter with Plan A? Plan B = backup deals that started at least 2 months ago.

_____

_____

_____

65

Compensation Plans that have 3 measures
to it outperform plans with fewer or more.
—Chris Cabrera (CEO, Xactly Corp.)
via Diane Updyke

_____

_____

_____

Sales stats should be open and viewable to all on your team and to those that support the team. It forms a common language and allows conversations to talk about improvements vs. arguing facts.

Diane Updyke
http://aha.pub/BuildingYourSalesTeam

Share the AHA messages from this book socially by going to
http://aha.pub/BuildingYourSalesTeam

Section IV

Operations—It Just IS

How do I best ramp the sales model? How do I best grow the team? How do I add efficiency and not just reps? Operations is the function you think about before you need to; otherwise, you'll spend a disproportionate amount of time catching up on organizational soundness.

Watch this video:
http://aha.pub/BuildingYourSalesTeamS4

66

There are over 700 vendors in the salestech landscape. Pick no more than YOU or SalesOPS can manage + a limit of spend/rep. Likely, 5 to start, don't grow past 10.

_____

_____

_____

67

What's more important than the Sales Stack or a particular feature set in your tech stack is whether it integrates with your CRM. You and your team will not go to more than 1-2 portals.

_____

_____

_____

68

The goal is to balance the ratio: cost per rep of technology investment to the decrease in time spent for non-selling activities. No right answer, but you'll get a baseline and learn how much your ops team can tolerate.

_____

_____

_____

69

Divide what you measure and what you manage. You can measure anything you put in CRM. You can dashboard to 15 graphs, reasonably. However, you will likely only manage to 5 points.

_____

_____

_____

70

Sales stats should be open and viewable to all on your team and to those who support the team. It forms a common language and allows conversations to talk about improvements vs. arguing facts.

_____

_____

71

Ensure that all your hard work in building your lead funnel doesn't crash on the front lines from lack of process and consistency. Roll up your sleeves to monitor and structure the last mile of engagement.
—MariAnne Vanella
(CEO of The Vanella Group, Inc.)
via Diane Updyke

72

There are lies, damn lies, and statistics.
—Mark Twain.
Don't underestimate a good gut check as a bumper.

73

We all run out of GEO territories as the sales team grows. What's next? Named Accts/Revenue/Verticals/Deal Size/ABC Grades. It WILL hurt. It won't be even. Reps will grumble. Make it defensible and equally unfair.

_____

_____

_____

74

When hiring is no longer adding linear revenue, add efficiency, not headcount. Outside parties can bring fresh ideas and studies.

_____

_____

_____

75

Take care to nourish and develop
the ecosystem: your partners and
implementers. They spread the word and
highlight the impact of your
product to customers.

_____

_____

_____

76

Improving Efficiency is a Sales Ops game. It's like an industrial technologist where they can see the holes between the systems and team structure.

_____

_____

_____

77

Greater sales effectiveness comes from sales ops (getting more out of your systems), sales enablement (getting more out of your people), and culture (getting more out of communications).

_____

_____

_____

Training is learning WHAT to do, Practice is learning HOW to own it, and Culture will make the team WANT to keep at it.

Diane Updyke
http://aha.pub/BuildingYourSalesTeam

Share the AHA messages from this book socially by going to
http://aha.pub/BuildingYourSalesTeam

Section V

Support Structures Complete You

These are the fastest growing segments in the modern sales organization. They are specialists. They keep their eye on every ball in your operation. They see stuff you don't. Treat them like gold.

Watch this video:
http://aha.pub/BuildingYourSalesTeamS5

78

The Sales manager is the one who grounds you when you miss curfew. Sales Enablement is the one who says, "How can we help you avoid missing curfew next time?"
—Misha Mcpherson
(CEO of HumbleGritSales) via Diane Updyke

_____

_____

_____

79

When do you need sales enablement?
As a concept, from your 1st non-founder
salesperson. As a hire, when you have 10+
reps with growth. As an org, when you have
predictable, consistent growth.
—Misha McPherson
(CEO of HumbleGritSales) via Diane Updyke

_____

_____

_____

80

Onboarding week 1: How does your new hire feel? Onboarding week 2: What does your new hire know? —Misha McPherson (CEO of HumbleGritSales)
via Diane Updyke

_____

_____

_____

81

A strong team requires tight alignment between Sales Ops and Sales Mgt. Managers can't hold reps accountable to a process they don't understand, and the best operational plan is wasted on reps who are not held accountable.
—Taft Love
(Global Dir of Sales Dev at SmartRecruiters)
via Diane Updyke

82

Sales Enablement isn't your clean-up crew. Use them to be proactive, not reactive.
—Misha McPherson
(CEO of HumbleGritSales)
via Diane Updyke

83

Sales Development Reps will be the first line of defense; they will learn why people want to talk to you. They are your entry and your future. They are a top investment. Treat them like it.

_____

_____

_____

84

#VariablesMatter in developing a sales model. Just as you can't borrow your neighbor's pants and assume they'll fit, you can't just borrow another company's model and think it will work for your culture/market/customers. —Trish Bertuzzi (President of The Bridge Group, Inc.) via Diane Updyke

_____

_____

_____

85

Sales Development is the glue between sales and marketing. Regardless of % marketing drives for inbound leads, SDRs lead the efforts on lists, buyer persona, messaging, and content. —Sally Duby (West Coast General Manager at The Bridge Group, Inc.) via Diane Updyke

_____

_____

_____

86

WHO should bring your powerful message to the market? Answer: Not the least experienced among us to take on the hardest part of the sales process, your SDRs. Yet, we often ask them to. —Sally Duby (West Coast General Manager at The Bridge Group, Inc.) via Diane Updyke

_____

_____

_____

87

Put the Customer first. But that doesn't always mean give them what they ask for. Henry Ford said: "If I asked my customers what they want, they would say a faster horse." Find their pain. Give them what they need.
—Joe Payne (President and CEO at Code42) via Diane Updyke

_____

_____

_____

88

Customers may come for your product, but
they stay for the people. Never lose sight
of that in marketing, sales, service, and
support. Your network is your net worth.
—Paul Teshima (CEO of Nudge.ai)
via Diane Updyke

_____

_____

_____

89

Why should you care about your customers? Because it's tied to your revenue focus, and at some point, you'll make more money with customers than in new business. I've seen it as early as around the $17 million mark.

_____

_____

90

Implement Customer Service before you think you need it. Do it at least 6 months before your first contract expires. Don't abuse your SEs. Get and incent actual Customer Success.

_____

_____

_____

91

The way to build authentic relationships is through shared passions and interests. Not title, role, industry, etc. Find something you both are interested in, it can be business or personal, and build from there.
—Paul Teshima (CEO of Nudge.ai)
via Diane Updyke

92

Training is kinda like a shower; you may have done it before, but it's a good idea to take one once in a while.

93

When does training have tangible results?
When you can do your own demos and
omit 2 calls in every sales cycle.

_____

_____

_____

94

I do encourage individuals to constantly
experiment and take calculated risks with
a few chips — those are the kind of failures
I call "tuition." If you don't pay it, you are
probably not learning. —Amit Bendov
(CEO and Co-founder of Gong.io)
via Diane Updyke

_____

_____

95

Training is learning WHAT to do, Practice is learning HOW to own it, and Culture will make the team WANT to keep at it.

_____

_____

_____

96

Don't just train your salespeople to be like your best salesperson today. Train your salespeople to be your best salespeople tomorrow. They need different skills. You are welcome. Is there anything else I can help you with?
—Misha Mcpherson
(CEO of HumbleGritSales)
via Diane Updyke

_____

_____

Marketing believes it produces 80% of the sales funnel; sales believes it's closer to 40% of the funnel. Somewhere in the middle is the truth. Moral is, sales leaders teach reps to fish.

Diane Updyke
http://aha.pub/BuildingYourSalesTeam

Share the AHA messages from this book socially by going to
http://aha.pub/BuildingYourSalesTeam

Section VI

Sales and Marketing Alignment— It's the WHOLE World

The Buyer's Journey is a delicate handoff from marketing to sales. The language, the stages, and the readiness of a prospect must be strictly defined; plus, the systems that perform the tasks must be tightly integrated. My best moment as a sales leader who coordinated with marketing was the time we set our common yearly goals in twenty minutes because we knew how to speak the same language. We knew what stretch it would take from each of us to move the business forward. This section takes you through the arc of building a sales funnel, getting marketing to work effectively on sales' behalf, and what courtesies you need to extend back to marketing to make the whole funnel stronger.

Watch this video:
http://aha.pub/BuildingYourSalesTeamS6

97

Sales is the internal customer of Marketing. Start with the belief that Marketing feeds Sales, then figure out a common Funnel language.

98

Marketing believes it produces 80% of the sales funnel; sales believes it's closer to 40% of the funnel. Somewhere in the middle is the truth. Moral is, sales leaders teach reps to fish.

99

Sales and marketing misalignment means missed opportunities. Both teams will have interactions with the customer at various points of the journey. Consistency in message, content, tone, experience, etc. is imperative. —Olivier Gachot (CSO of NewVoiceMedia) via Diane Updyke

---

100

Marketing is your BFF if you teach sales to partially feed themselves and to funnel insights back to marketing.

101

As Sales expects funnel metrics from Marketing, so should Marketing expect that from Sales. Agree on an SLA for turnaround time on qualified lead followup. For my teams, 48 hours was reasonable. If you can tighten it to 24 hrs, good on ya.

102

To narrow the free-for-all of selling in early markets focus on a market/industry segment, but never quit testing the fringe of your targets.

103

Track your whole pipeline, from interest to suspect to prospect to sales cycle to won/lost. Sales may not own it all. It's a good lesson in collaboration.

_____

_____

_____

104

ICP is a guess, market education, and the observation of needs. You are educated enough today to make the first guess. Paying customers will turn that guess into your ICP.

_____

_____

_____

105

Sometimes, there isn't a list for your particular ICP. One time, my company's ICP was determined to be a "smart marketer." Where's THAT list? We had to use Discovery to determine if a prospect was a fit for us.

_____

_____

_____

106

ICPs beget target lists of WHOM has a need for your product. Discovery questions beget WHICH of those targets is a fit for your sales process in your timeframe.

_____

_____

_____

107

The most important thing I've learned is that brand isn't just marketing. It isn't a veneer you apply to your business.
It's not a side-show, it's the whole show.
—Pat Nicholson
(CMO, Deserve, Inc and Advisor)
via Diane Updyke

_____

_____

_____

108

Your Brand is a Promise. It's your Promise
to your customers. The best brands arise
from companies that make a compelling
promise and deliver on that promise
in compelling ways. Think BMW:
the Ultimate Driving Machine.
—Pat Nicholson
(CMO, Deserve, Inc and Advisor)
via Diane Updyke

_____

_____

_____

109

Your brand is more than just logos, messaging, and advertising. Great companies strive to make sure their marketing, products, business model, and service model are all aligned to back up their Promise.
—Pat Nicholson
(CMO, Deserve, Inc and Advisor)
via Diane Updyke

110

Branding is hard. It's not an exact science. It requires finding. SaaS startups often wait to develop branding until sales has enough customers. That's hard on sales.

111

The more branding that can be created and proliferated to the market, the easier and more efficient sales can be. At first, it's a delicate balance to keep from overly relying on Sales to be your only marketing.

_____

_____

_____

You collect ideas, concerns, inputs from in front of the desk. You document them from behind the desk. You profess and share them in internal meetings. It's a tripod of activities to generate new ideas.

Diane Updyke
http://aha.pub/BuildingYourSalesTeam

Share the AHA messages from this book socially by going to
http://aha.pub/BuildingYourSalesTeam

Section VII

Managing the Team =
Help Me Help You

While we manage the systems of our business uniformly, we motivate people individually. So, how can we manage a group of individuals fairly and get them all moving in the same direction? This section informs how to manage the team, get close to the action, hone your managerial skills, and instill the key aspects of culture.

Watch this video:
http://aha.pub/BuildingYourSalesTeamS7

112

There is the journey a Manager takes to become a Leader. This section explores how you manage through being their Friend, to being a Hardhead, to knowing stuff, to evolving into a Mentor.

_____

_____

_____

113

Frontline managers advocate for what are the obstacles in your reps' common sales cycle and work to remove them. Your team is running well if you can spend more time removing sales obstacles and with customers than on HR matters.

_____

_____

_____

114

The higher up your managerial position, the more you are beholden to decisions that favor the company.

115

Your 30-day PTO test: A sign of a great manager is that they can take 30 days off and everything will work just fine. It means that they have hired the right people and have the processes in place.
—Amit Bendov
(CEO and Co-founder of Gong.io)
via Diane Updyke

116

Challenge yourself on coaching to get 75% of your team to 100% Club.

_____

_____

_____

117

Opportunity coaching that starts AFTER solution validation is a coach calling plays after the game has been decided. —Matt Cameron (Sales Management Program Leader at SaaSy Sales Management) via Diane Updyke

_____

_____

_____

118

You collect ideas, concerns, inputs from in front of the desk. You document them from behind the desk. You profess and share them in internal meetings. It's a tripod of activities to generate new ideas.

_____

_____

119

As a leader, you can feel things from a call that your reps may not intuit. That story you hear can spread to an entire team.
That's a superpower.

_____

_____

_____

120

Know your metrics as a manager on how much time you spend behind a desk vs. in front of it and/or with customers. It'll help prioritize your schedule for the coming week.

_____

_____

_____

121

Your manager would like to know how much time you are on calls and with reps. If you know that metric, it'll help you justify other things you want to do.

_____

_____

_____

122

When do you separate Hunters from Farmers? Before Customers are the majority of your business.

_____

_____

_____

123

When should a Customer move to the Account Manager group? First: After the Hunter has enough time to land & expand, but BEFORE they take it for granted.

_____

_____

_____

124

When do Hunters own the account, and when does it turn over to Farmers? It arcs depending on the stage. It usually settles at 12 months for turnover with lots of experimentation.

_____

_____

_____

125

Questions to ask: Are customers one and done? Are first deals POCs? Which group will manage to expansion?
Are these strategic accounts?

_____

_____

_____

126

Discipline is broken down into what you schedule and do every month, every week, every day. Prosperity is what you get when you do it religiously.

_____

_____

_____

127

A Sales Rep with longevity shows curiosity, discipline, a good use of data, adoption of tools, and timely sharing of content. It's who they just are day and night.

_____

_____

_____

128

Pipeline building is the equivalent of making your bed so you can comfortably slip into it later.

_____

_____

_____

129

Discipline is filling your pipeline when times are good.

_____

_____

_____

130

Each Rep should map their own individual
close rate. It will tell you how much needs
to be added to your pipeline, which tells you
how hard you need to work today.

_____

_____

_____

131

Some believe that an ex-employee will
always be part of the corporate family;
some believe they are dead to you once
they leave—one approach can give
you folks who'll work for you again.

_____

_____

_____

132

Culture isn't a Strategy, it's a habit that shows in formal and informal ways. Strategy is a dictum; Culture takes time and a wave swell to move.

_____

_____

_____

133

Culture is an organism. Take regular & anonymous surveys to check on it. Get a bead on the overall mood. It doesn't mean you do all they ask.

_____

_____

_____

134

What do managers really want from the managers who work for them? To win, to make your manager look good, and to make life easier for others.

_____

_____

_____

Career paths are for B players. Career paths attract talent, which is good. But A players simply say yes when opportunity knocks. And opportunities come to top talent. — Bill Binch (CRO, Pendo.io)

Diane Updyke
http://aha.pub/BuildingYourSalesTeam

Share the AHA messages from this book socially by going to http://aha.pub/BuildingYourSalesTeam

Section VIII

General Skills and Tips—Read These! They Have Some of the Best Advice

Sometimes, there is information that doesn't fit into a category but is so useful, you will own it like a mantra. I'll leave you with general wisdom and useful bits of knowledge in business and in life.

Watch this video:
http://aha.pub/BuildingYourSalesTeamS8

135

On your Career, if you're not setting career or life goals, then you're just along for the ride and someone else is dictating your path.
—John Barrows
(CEO of JBarrows Sales Training)
via Diane Updyke

136

Career paths are for B players. Career paths attract talent, which is good. But A players simply say yes when opportunity knocks. And opportunities come to top talent.
—Bill Binch (CRO, Pendo.io)
via Diane Updyke

137

Career failures are overrated. There are infinitely more ways to fail than to succeed. Hire people who have had successful runs and know what winning looks like.
—Amit Bendov
(CEO and Co-founder of Gong.io)
via Diane Updyke

138

No matter the strategy, the sales plays, the account plans, and the discipline, it still gets down to a deal at a time. It matters the deals you choose to be in and how EACH ONE is executed.

139

John Chambers once said that life is all about good lighting and good timing. Take advantage of both when you can.
—Neil Callahan
(Co-founder of Pilot Growth Equity)
via Diane Updyke

_____

_____

_____

140

Sometimes, it's good to hear the perspective of another generation, even if it's fresh and not yet seasoned: Charity is when you help someone once or a few times, Social Justice is when you teach the steps to change their life.
—Kyra Updyke, 16
via Diane Updyke

_____

_____

_____

bout the Author

iane Updyke has grown over six B2B SaaS software sales ams with positive outcomes to companies like BEA, Oracle, d Marketo. The transition from server-based selling to SaaS ves her a broad base of sales methodologies and team growth actices, especially at the early stages of Martech and social atform industries. Diane has focused half of her consulting on les and marketing alignment and sales funnel development, hich has helped over ten startups find traction and growth in the les funnel. She still loves the game. Currently, Diane is advising d consulting on top-leveling sales teams for tech and non-tech dustries. She has also been featured on panels and webcasts, te the Sales Lead Management Channel. Diane also sits on the ard of the local chapter for the National Charity League, an ganization that directs mother-daughter teams in community rvice and leadership.

THiNKaha has created AHAthat for you to share content from this book.

- Share each AHA message socially:
  http://aha.pub/BuildingYourSalesTeam

- Share additional content: https://AHAthat.com

- Info on authoring: https://AHAthat.com/Author

CPSIA information can be obtained
at www.ICGtesting.com
Printed in the USA
BVHW011725050122
625213BV00016B/34

9 781616 9931